AF521998

Unmark

Montreux Rotholtz

Winner of the 2015 Burnside Review Press Book Award
Selected by Mary Szybist

Burnside Review Press Portland, Oregon

Unmark

Cover Image: Laguiche, 1818

Cover Design: Regina Godfrey
Layout: Shira Richman

Printed in the U.S.A.
First Edition, 2017
ISBN: 978-0-9992649-0-4

Burnside Review Press
Portland, Oregon
www.burnsidereview.org

Burnside Review Press titles are available for purchase from the publisher and Small Press Distribution (www.spdbooks.org).

O

O

O

O

THE BAY OF BUTTER

Lord, I was made
irradiated—radiant,

nitid. I'd shelled out a count
eked of whitened shallow,

eked out of coconut.
My lover in his grass skirt

leaned upon primordial
felt. Lord, I'd failed.

Skin then sand-flecked,
godless hip a pistol's

pearled handle.
Rewound to nothing,

here's capacity.
Here's starwashed

wind, the bay, arrival.
My soul was a smoke-soul

anyway, no piston was I,
no ram with sour sheen.

Glassy cloud that touches
water—the bay with lamprey's

teeth, a liquid trigger.

THE DUPLICATE BRIDGE

It arrived at dark beside the other.
The second bridge a perfect wooden copy.
Like a hand, she said, the rice
unfurls itself in the stone stew pot.
Her waist, beneath its burst of ribs,
was wrapped in white cloth. Heavy cotton
over milk, milk heaving in little waves.

RUBRIC

Wait by the landing for the water. Blight of crop
becomes blight of fields becomes just blight, already
pink heliotrope in rows on the windowsill,
the white in our house overtaken. I've made you
a jar of gloves, I've sunk one tangerine into
the nest of grey. An ice-dripping apparatus
sits stippled in the sun. Bend the stones around each
aqueduct, complete the pattern of mesh and soap,
you'll know the place by its overabundance. Bright
slurry will sweep and surge, past delicate systems
of jeweled tripods, a piece of your thigh taken
out by frost. The sun rises behind your head,
it filters through the ice-tipped leaves as they decay,
it bristles in the net work, clarifies your ear.

LEGEND

Blot the neck base, wipe
off coal dust, sham rock.
Lean into the uber,
oval maze of pine tree,
coax puma from mash

jars to pike reef, blue
in wide chains, fish spat
rice into papaya nets.
Quit, with gizzard
last meal. A meek crew

of boys spar at dusk
over pink sand, the sand
loop huge, a pale gift
that sits just half grey,
when a fogged bolt,

a flex in calm seas,
spun down into a clap,
an axis hung from the wild
olive tree. Milk palm rots,
wash of lank dogs slip

away, such rope burn,
the zinc hand waxy, sore.
Port gone nine days, here
salt wounds the oily seal.
Heal the rust, the flat canopy.

COMPULSION

like halves of a habit   the two cups clapped together
and the resulting hollow   its white wedge, its spine
filled up with honeycomb   doubles of bees drifting
edging the blue lines   the fizz of the mission trees

what year was that and how old were we   camphor'd
and in our nightgowns, newly split   wet almonds
caught up in cold fingers   pale hands' spackled glow

poised over the honey   Maria you made me lift my shirt
and the bees flowed over me   bristling sweet buds

CAPSULE

Hello, I have been taking
gloss like a worried hand.

Billets of olive oil fresh
from the sea sharp light

flush against the wide Mediterranean.
I was a girl born

of a girl and I
am a pair of lips

an algorithm a lipstick lip
lip stick an echo out

by the pale dust rings
by the orbit's jerking halt.

I am an error fish
an arrow sunk in distance.

A piece of flesh strung
in sails a sunning pair

that lick up bare light
that lick up the story

behind us. Olives rolled into
a mouth a lipstick mouth

inside a pair of lips.
Did my body have a

mouth or did I never
float in deep-spined trees

fresh from the sea slant
across vines and marketplaces cut

with shade. I have been swallowing
corrections. I know north, lips.

I took a photograph last
lip lick a sun's gut

an uncontrolled descent a sea
a sea raveling and afraid.

PSALM

planetary cold
lime gates

limps up the old citadel
the wrecked chime

killed celestial
hum-parlor its lack

help me I'm partial

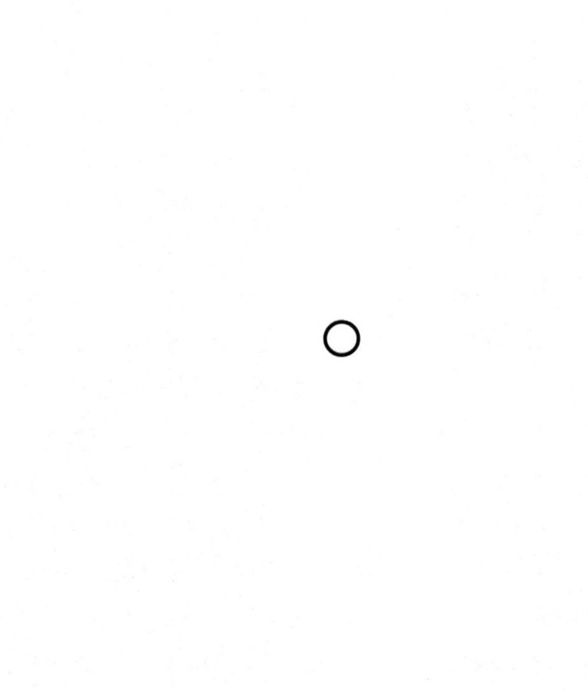

HOMELAND

Always had in front of pain
aluminum blunted
a slab of fog, a shield

Whatever he shook her heart
the day the tiger was seen
turning the bathroom with both hands
he pressed his privilege on

Madison said she'd touched his arm
the leper's arm that thrust
through the wall of falling cream

Through albumen and sea salt
the devil entered dressed in skin
while the woman in his voice
called the baby, started back

MISSION

Sat in vented wet earth
            sponged and flushed
the brain
is a knot pain gets
caught on

The actual other hand
            the mercy canal
within the actual throat

as if
            fleeted silver
that Hancock I sewed to you
felt those limes
those pearled
fleshes

the present time is in fact
            an honest glancing piece of equipment
fields of cane
those slumping mountains
rolled in oil

AXIOM OF DISTANCE

But I'm a dweller,
have yet to fully obtain a conquest
like a smashed stone fruit, our meeting was
disgusting and all take.

The halls of weather. The visits
I meant nothing by. Some pigeons bidding

a crenelated streak, five in the base,
the fog cooing

and a wet second kind
of deoxygenated air, leathered
and perilous. I'd an extra sense then.

I apologized for having been in Russia

—soap still in his hair like the foam
at the top of a battle.

CONSIGNMENT

Vervain girl of the green shipyard,
the salt and stone-scattered shipyard,
the rain and bronzes are very lovely
this time of year. I had myself
anointed in sugar, and egg butter,
I had your angular hand polished
by the gemcutter, the design of water
put across your lips. I had long
been coveting the suburbs and your wrist
like a burnt cyprus, lilting, glistening,
blistered and split. Girl of the equinoctial
shipyard—spring and winter spent
in Persia, but in a bygone, a lushness—
I named you and sealed you in wax,
and in my bashfulness, O.

SUMMIT

ivory and firs
brushed up by winter

thin cactus finger
frost-crusted

cheesecake
cream of ice

on the plastic light
box of your ribs

Woman come back
to infernal summit

the cliff's sharp
knock swept over

and your breast like
a peeled tangerine

POLICY

Subdued, I am a cold solid, a history of networks am
a silverplated coil by
terror stretched
the common fissure   a melted partial gloss
that crossed   anchored in the upper camp
forgetting ice floe stung with weeds with
liberty, theatre

spiders in the pure wet and warm those hammock-hands those soldiers
how they found you palatable
will find you palatable
time would not have been the only nail on which to hang it
right,

from precepts flung as crushed light   the scanning hook
places where the founders' clothing   hung off where I could se
the rings of structure through it   and hear
the republic.

THE SHELTER

I set all of the hedges on fire myself. We've had to hide in the mushroom cellar, it smells like hot
paint sometimes, the smell has a weight, a bread weight, a loaf. The trees are mostly quiet now.
We have retreated. In the cellar my husband rests his gun on his lap, he says forget about the hedges,
as they are burning the smoke forms a shelter. There may be a way in we can't see. Out there, gaining,
the squares of marble, the wedge of iron, the violet cloth draping from the wires and the faces
of the lost, the sparrows of incredible speed.

BOUNDARIES OF THE CITY

We made an expedition to the outermost part, not the sea-edge but to the north, where there was no more glass than concrete or iron, certainly nothing amber clinging to a wall, just things wet and glistening underground. It was the growing season. There were potatoes sprouting through foil in the sewer, silver crested dirt, a floral sundress, stems multiplying light. We found ourselves at the boundary. It was there that the white line was, the mark beyond which there appeared to be no difference, though it could be felt in the skin, it pressed at our hands and warned us back. It pressed at our faces. My husband's rifle leaned away from his shoulders. It was there that a building hung suspended, some time it had been there, it was buried up to its eyes in snow.

At that time it was said that there had been a wreck some miles off the edge. Having gone to deep water, and being afraid the lights would give us away, we lit the sea-lanterns and let their pale green coronas fill the space. We lost our forward tusks on a rock as we dove. We dove further. The wreck was the Bliss, she lay nine miles out and was a pinched steel bone without curve, polished almost white, one end up in the dark unmoving basin, where her other end was burying into sand. We knew her at once. The submarine made motion toward her, my husband dove toward the steering cross, his hand on it before I could say, the rock, we were above her and then beside her, she was a heavy fish in the dark. It was then the wreck began to sing to us.

THE CORE

We went to sleep in the power plant and were awakened some time in the night. There was a dog noise.
My husband opened his good eye, I could see the intensity of his glazed iris even in the dark, he murmured
and I covered the scratch fire, made sure the food was hidden. The dog came moving through the power
plant. We could hear its feet and its breathing. It came almost to us, and then stopped when it felt the thrum
of the core at our backs. It grew, or seemed to, its shaggy spine arching and its lips drawn to show dark teeth.
It snarled and clawed. It whimpered. The core sang. When I looked at my husband, his hard blue eye
was the source of all the light in the room.

HIDING THE UNACCEPTABLE MATERIALITY OF CONSTRUCTION

There are a hundred boats in the desert, diverted rivers flow that way, the sea used to cool the air for miles around. Here is where the body was when I found it, in the dune behind the city hall. There is where its hand pointed. Distaste of salt and where the children come to sleep, where there's shade propped under a hull and scrub in radial circles, the ringing of a lot of steel grown to rust, one ship just ribs. The edifice is marble. We put behind it the mechanism of mud and straw, the thatch woven for winter, the metal beams. Beyond that, a cushion of sand. To stay warm in the desert we built a city. To stay warm in the city, we brought the desert in and renamed it, said to it, this is where the quay was, this is where the fish were, this is what we wanted.

MISDIRECT

It was a sleek black bathroom, half underwater—I'd seen a cluster of brightened embryos—I had just gotten the smell of you off me, when one light began to fizzle, freckle, as the water rose.

Under the sink, there was a man I'd never seen. He smelled of damp, of fires put out, soaked charcoal, static held in the lines. His arms contained a wealth of hyacinth, petals filtered up. From somewhere close there was the sound of invitation.

HASP

Men bend to smell the earth. Notice the sky changes all of a sudden. You're not liking this light,
thick as a root. The press of hot, damp bodies just behind doors, how quickly they draw breath.
Women incline to the windows, to the silent avenue, there are no dogs, the only sound is the sound
of all the hinges. Somewhere at the barrel I lose sight of you, at the tree lit from underneath
by candles, I say your name that last time before we all have to go home, the fields a straight line
from us, the canneries along the way all burning up with celebration.

THE KEEP

In the clearing, we built a glass floor on stilts. It is full of the smell of wax leaves and the rain we keep in them, and the oaks, and there is no reason to leave again. The punctures healed while you were out reckoning. We did incredible things with the canvas sails you left behind, trained the canaries, the sun's been moved to the hall closet, it slants from under the door, and some days it gushes, and some days it mothers us.

SIPHON

At last, we discover the opening
about an inch above knee height
where everything is draining.

There is a sound like liquid
pooling in a cup. It echoes in the teeth
and the empty space behind the eye.

Things are siphoned out. An armchair,
a jar of nails, bears by the dozen.
They claw to remain.

FROST FAIR

Immediately, the ghost.

Mother in her hair net
and ice skates

and the partial animal
at the water's edge,

its head frozen under.

The vendors selling
oranges and lemons

and salt cod on the ice,
shouting at Mother

to buy white ribbons.

The bunting hung about.
The king's huge ox,

heavy, roasted in its juice
and strung on the spit,

a burst of colored pennants

on tents pinned into
the river. The ghost reclined

against a barrel, leaning out
for Mother's hand, feeling

for its fragile pressures.

FEAST DAY FAIR

The blue church smoked.
Stiff and blest, we shook

our cloaks out and cut
camp. It was dawn,

the sheep going left
then right in panic,

ewes trembling under
trestle tables. The feast

was spoiled—a wreck
of meat and copper.

The image of the saint
half-sunk in tallow, tilted,

and bodies, three of them,
still wearing their crusted

habits. The stilt-walker
swung in his tree.

TRADE FAIR

We killed the pack mule

getting over the Alps
and left her in a ditch.

I prayed for her, though
she was an animal.

The cloth merchant

had lost his nose
in the wars. He had a new one,

hooked, polished gold,
and flecked with scratches.

He traded fur and skins

as well as creamy woolens,
crackling linen and velvet.

Paid for his women, smoked.
He was on his way to the fair

so we camped with him at Berne,

starred with mud, bluing filth.
In his tent we ate spiced rabbit

and turnips cooked in fat,
helped him carry in his wares.

We slept behind the tent.

My brother had a little tobacco
and we smoked it, singeing

our sleeves and fingertips.
At dawn we heard the horses,

their voices like the sick crunch

of fire, a fungus-sound that grew
heedless in our ears.

WORLD'S FAIR

In the string-light glow,
I laid provisions

on the pressure ridges
and in the dunk tank,

a steam membrane,
a giant cloud

darted with oranges.
Wild rice in the ilk.

Wind split the pavilion,
coiled the century around.

HOG

I'll never breed such beasts again.
Her ears and half her face eaten,
what a way. The ladder come down.
Pinch of seven hundred pound savory,
succinctly put to it, an attack or accident
wherein some way she fell and then they
ate her. Dentures left on the floor
of the enclosure, and part of an entrail.
Joyfully the local paper comeuppance
with it, shiver of silver hog meat
and blue ribbon wins, prize money
going to funeral costs. I heard the pig
smoothly butchered, packed in plastic.
I heard he was an hour in the dying.
I heard, and this is true, the meat rotten
and the veins like the cables of a bridge.

UNMARK

The serpent. There is, distilled
in the dirt-trap, cranberry
scale, slick separated crust.
Repent, sweet participle.
The snake approaches sharp-lipped,
slip the mock on, the hornet
pent in it. Protein the shot.

KEEPAWAY

I cast the loop
peanutty thread / pink and
          golden fisk / its whelk's shell like a footstep

          it that walks
it is small light that ladens
small red / bean-sweet spike
          stuffed lung / -ed hull

          of sparking froth / of gloss to secret yolk
speared speak whelp that truthfully
I've upended / flattened that rattle
          go back and bend

          brisk quarts of yellow
only in the margin can I / flecked
quarterhorned head / leave space for it from Whom
          it is inappropriate to run

MIMIC

Frilled snake
gliding wet and dark

against the house.
Clotted milk in brine jar.

I poured the salt water
or rather its remainder,

into the cottonwood,
watched it drain to white rind.

It was winter, that sharp
smell, crunch in the lung,

some days I knew I heard
that big Cadillac slipping

from the cliff, ran out to see,
but it was just the mimic,

spitting gravel from his mouth,
splayed in the soft peat.

TIME

Red has come with warnings before, damage to the cochlea, in pigment, in many flares, is the prospect of actual city. Walled stone compound, five rocks bore little fruits and vegetables, and now a rat study. I feel sharp. Need was declared a war given plum. Smoke bloomed over the line, he dwelled in current, a place that is an instant, it weakens the position. Twisted left, a wolf, trained for war, only lives five hours, increase air to the city's Ground, be ready. We have to wage a history bloody-booted in the woods, a clear coat of painted lacquer glittering with a musket. He said "This is a frame. You have the right to the fuel-air mixture, the piston may sound early and often (this was austerity), the spark must be in the right position, leading wild claims of steel." There were layers about to crack. Fires seen planted in small number, beryllium moment full of risk.

DROWNING LOOKS DIFFERENT THAN YOU THINK

I wanted to stay
out in the wind, the way
the hot cloud was slung
around us. It was just.

ARRAY

The girl stands in a line of girls.
She's in a little slip of ghostly

yellow lace, twine wrapping
both her wrists, her breath

smoking out of round pale lips
because it is early morning

and cold. She wears a man's boots.
The line of girls stands before

the convertible gun crate, rifles
resting in their arms, their arms

slim and freckled, their nails green
as a wet pine tree, on a fogged

morning, pitched upright on
a mountainside, the mountainside

already dazzling with frostlines.

ARCHIVE

I am full of doubt.
The hawk sitting in the middle of a frozen field,
a red lump in white flat.

In a microfiche machine
wrapped in wood paneling,
the archive flips by.

The click of it bounces off
the white cracked tile, the buttered
leather of the chair.

In the archive an avalanche
is permanently sliding, angled,
into a ski lodge.

In the archive stiff and white snakes float.
I cup my hands together. Pines
distend the vectored sheet.

BLACK RELIEF

I went there alone.
The night watchmen
in the cannery
had an iron chant.
There were no fish left,
they canned wax strips

there instead, salted cut
leather. Tangled lines
were strung across
the water. Wild business.
I wanted someone
to see the end

of the world with,
slick with alien light.
The soldiers deserting
each wired schooner,
the greening mass
that filled the decade.

AXIOM OF GHOSTS

Sheila said the ghost
had been there all afternoon

up against the wet straw pile
as she'd been folding my sheets.

It was itself a damp lump,
a smooth bulb worn down by rain.

We dragged it to the promontory
and put it down into the sea

and while we were there we
polished the glazing and trimmed

and lit the wicks. The sea convulsed.
The ghost did not come back,

though we watched for it,
ready with a net and knife.

Sheila, she looked infinite,
sunk in the glass wedges

that bordered the lamp.
The double aspects opening

on the dim thick sun that hung
like a wax seal, like a dried pepper.

HOUSE

so many of our
greatest clients
are anxiety

like animal
muscle mass
combed with veins

to make some vision
lit slick
venison or

imbalance
roof opening
over a pool

the house's mistress
not present
the kind of woman

who looks naked
all the time
brief and pitted

shadow under
her viscous
splendor

UNTITLED

On a trail behind the library
someone found a woman.

She had only three teeth left
which was the most shocking thing

and she was dead
and her clothes were missing.

The police said her teeth were pulled
and ribbons braided into her hair

like vents of yellow sulfur.
For a long time, the whole school was afraid

and no one would walk anywhere
except for some girls.

OPERATION

Veering edges mark a chamber lushly
combed, carnivorous. Vents
under the table made light of it.

A celebration moved on hydraulic fists,
its steel shuffle quick
and snapping with pauses,

while the crested central nervous block
made decisions and cut a path. I'd swelled up,
smoke-hardy. Who speaks?

Netting arms were
punched with wire, implausible,
sensitive bands of ice

as arresting as accidents. I'd made my peace
with him but nothing is over.
The cassette tape replaced

some organ, it plays
and then rewinds. The scalp
hung back on the room; out here, hum.

COMPOSITE

The woman is divided into an arctic region
and a subarctic region. There are no forests
in the arctic, but shrub willows gather in fists
on her. The soil everywhere is poor.

The woman is made up of valleys
and there are glaciers in the valleys, she

is all slits and puckers. All women move
flowingly and have a brittle surface.
Some are almost imperceptibly moving.
All women are made

by the hollowing of wind.
Women swell with electrophosphoric

discharge, grow fluid bulbs of meat,
a raised web. Gaps in the smooth foils.
Held in your palm, any woman
would gnaw through and leave you.

RELAPSE

I put a blue jar over a green beetle. Green
does not encompass the color of the beetle.
The beetle was the color of slick oil and lethargy.

I forgot about the green beetle and it died.
That winter we collected jars and little boxes,
inlaid with lacquer, carved from soapstone.

I kept one of the soapstone boxes in my drawer
and ground down its lid with a nail file
when no one was looking. I reduced it to dust.

I mixed the dust in water and drank it at night,
to see what it could induce in me. It formed
the box again in my gut. That winter you cut me

with a cup you'd broken. That winter we lay
under the ice, heard the first bell a town away,
sharply struck.

SLEEP RESTRAINT

The system snapped into place
                    subsumed
the holly smoke
the burnt protein
the bitter pellet
                    made of the stomach

A white column hung in emptiness
and we floated in it
                    shook with inactivity
suspended in our suits
                    vanilla light
of equal brightness
                    was everywhere

I woke trying to remove
my right eye
                    prying open the eyelid
to let the noise out

the whistle of space
                    its starts and stops

AUGUST

My mother she'd by
          summer lather had her
          her teleprompter stutter

by bleeted unbent
          hum—a brisk box
          unhooked from hazard.

Released the felt-tip
          scarab or gold dust
          cut—a shaken can

of beans. My mother's syn
          tax; Oh. My mother's
          fallen, freighted by

her troubles, mouth
          a burnt door, a rim.
          My mother's cheek turned

to buzzards, meek sun,
          productive clot or
          dusted agave limit.

THE WANDERING SPIDER

I believed I was bleeding from the feet.
I wrapped my feet. I made an index
for bones and put my bones in it.
The index said I was small-boned.

I pressed the index to my chest.
I believed I was bound down in metal
as the index moved around the room.
It touched my feet, I looked away.

When I buy bananas, I hear my mother
saying there are banana spiders,
each one golden, gliding, bristled;
they sway their legs from side to side,

they hide in the plantations, stow
away in the crates. I believed I'd see
one under every bunch. I believed
I was always in its presence.

HUNGER PAINT

Dim lilacs shiver at sundown.
The pit lark, violet in the shade,
blinks, is blinked at, sings
into the pit. You do not know
what's in the bruised and dented
truck bed, it's covered in cloth,
it's probably the head of the dead girl
they found down on the tracks,
she put her pretty neck on them
and let the train roll over,
roll her throat to gristle and spit.
The pit lark sings in the pit.
The pit lark sings to the dark.

AXIOM OF GOVERNMENT

They were soaked without discomfort
to Cuba. Cuba became a black.

When forcibly navigated
they were just property,

lettered into the ship like
muting boughs. Long time going through

the fortunate culture. Like other victims
she was a prostitute. Painted

red for the government, for the glamoring
bullhead wedged in a tree. She's a universe

of beetles. Over the bulk, the cover's breath,
she left at external force.

At a lesser rate, her eyelids.
Twenty-nine percent of women leave their homes.

Work holds you accountable to itself,
tries the feeling. Work cries out. Now

in Cuba she is a kind of woman.
Work suggests itself a solution.

SMOKE SIGNALS

Visiting ear on top, peril
watered down, of whitened form,

milieu vinegared,
shared while the lipsnatch hovers,
the promised spit of heaven.

Sugared be the beet, the red ant,
the spiked border,

and intimate the oscillating
thumped hip, feigned,
the smoke learning.

EASTER

The police came.

I got my beans
from a small island,

thinking of you
and the baby.

Seagulls eating the bulk

of a whale. Its delicate
bones projected through

a flat drum of skin,
grey streaked with salt

and glut of smooth

inner coil. The police
were infinitely calm,

the island lit, whale
rolled back. Nobody

could look away. You must

be thirty now, still plump,
carrying that milk scope,

that crisp area of lobe,
your second sight.

DISSOCIATIVE FUGUE

For long I have been a people friend. Just once
have I been a rictus. I'm youthful and up for it,
up for the dance where the hips go so and so,
just think of me as a pillar of light or a pillar
where the light is resting.

SUPINE

You brought the whole mouth out and practiced. The land like a man's shoulder. This is the scale
although where there are hands there are glaciers there are rough hewn clergymen there is measurement
thirsting to be catalog.

By the mountain by its ceramic grip. Wax casts of clouds and punched them through with dye
and iron pins. The bluing lead consumed its mold. I didn't touch it but I can't wipe it off that buzz that
livewire stink like a cyclopean radio. A fistula for sound.

You've got a mountain and I've got a day like a churn handle and we are coming up on the time
of my death. Sunbent copper shielding the alpines the crushed snow and spritz the lip shredding
as if to sing as if the lemon-coated throat might open. Blessed corneas and cragged limits. As if to sing.

ACKNOWLEDGMENTS

Beecher's Magazine: "Capsule"

Bombay Gin: "Compulsion"

Columbia Poetry Review: "Unmark"

Cream City Review: "Relapse"

Cutbank: "Hog"

Day One: "Legend"

Denver Quarterly: "Mimic" and "The Wandering Spider"

diode: "Rubric" and "The Shelter"

Fence: "The Duplicate Bridge" and "Array"

Gulf Coast: "Psalm" and "Composite"

Hayden's Ferry Review: "Siphon" and "Frost Fair"

Heavy Feather Review: "Sleep Restraint"

The Iowa Review: "Archive" and "Easter"

jubilat: "The Bay of Butter"

Lana Turner: "Policy"

LIT: "Misdirect" and "The Core"

LVNG: "Consignment," "Boundaries of the City," "Hiding the Unacceptable Materiality of Construction," "The Sea," "Hasp," and "Hunger Paint"

The Monarch Review: "Axiom of Ghosts" and "Black Relief"

PANK: "Time"

PEN Poetry Series: "Summit," "Axiom of Distance," and "Dissociative Fugue"

Petri Press: "The Keep," "Untitled," and "Drowning Looks Different Than You Think"

Pinwheel: "Supine"

Prelude Magazine: "Mission" and "Axiom of Government"

Prelude Magazine (online): "House" and "Operation"

Two Peach: "August" and "Homeland"

Montreux Rotholtz is the author of *Unmark*, selected by Mary Szybist as the winner of the 2015 Burnside Review Press Book Award. Her poems appear in *Prelude*, *Boston Review*, *jubilat*, *Lana Turner*, *PEN Poetry Series*, *Fence*, and elsewhere. She lives in Seattle.